Deadly Animals

Henry Brook

Designed by Tom Lalonde, Zöe Wray and Helen Edmonds

Illustrated by Staz Johnson and Ian McNee

Edited by Alex Frith

Animals experts: Dr. Margaret Rostron and Dr. John Rostron

Contents

Inside the safety of a shark cage, this wildlife photographer can get up close to a great white shark.

Deadly encounters

Almost all wild creatures, even the most powerful, try hard to avoid contact with people. A very few will actually hunt and kill them. But, when an encounter goes wrong, every animal in this book – big or small – can be deadly.

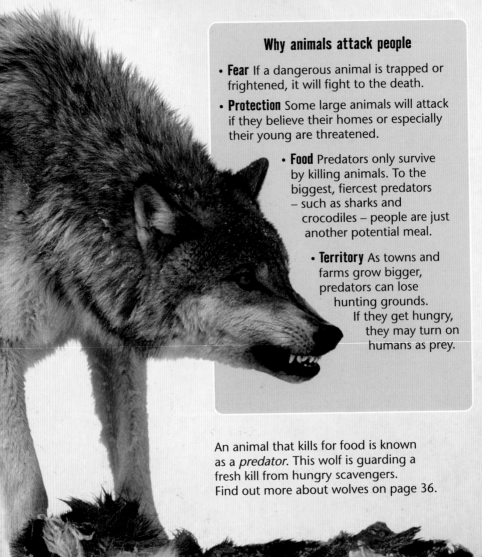

Why animals attack people

- **Fear** If a dangerous animal is trapped or frightened, it will fight to the death.
- **Protection** Some large animals will attack if they believe their homes or especially their young are threatened.
- **Food** Predators only survive by killing animals. To the biggest, fiercest predators – such as sharks and crocodiles – people are just another potential meal.
- **Territory** As towns and farms grow bigger, predators can lose hunting grounds. If they get hungry, they may turn on humans as prey.

An animal that kills for food is known as a *predator*. This wolf is guarding a fresh kill from hungry scavengers. Find out more about wolves on page 36.

Killing by numbers

The scariest animals don't cause the most harm. Most attacks are survivable, with the right medical attention. As this chart shows, it's the smallest creatures that cause the most deaths...

General animal type	Estimated human death toll per year*	Deadliest specific animal
Sharks	5-15	Great white shark
Jellyfish	around 50	Sea wasp (a type of box jellyfish)
Bees	50-200	Africanized honey bee
Lions	100	East African lion
Elephants	100-300	Asian elephant
Hippos	100-500	*Hippopotamus amphibius*
Crocodiles	1,000	Nile crocodile
Scorpions	3,000	Fattail scorpion
Snakes	20,000-100,000	Indian cobra
Mosquitoes	725,000-1.8 million	Malaria-carrying *Anopheles* mosquito

*Determining an exact death toll caused by one type of animal is very tough. These estimates were taken from research conducted by the *World Health Organization*, the *Bill Gates Foundation* and the *World Wildlife Fund*.

Wrath of the whale

In the 19th century, whaleships hunted sperm whales all across the Atlantic and Pacific oceans. These whales were targeted as a valuable source of oil for lamps.

In one exceptional case, an angry sperm whale took the fight to a crew of 20 men...

The whaleship *Essex* was in the middle of the Pacific when her crew sighted water spouts.

The captain sent three small boats after a pod of sperm whales. A harpooner balanced on the prow of each boat, ready to hook an animal.

One of the whales struck back, smashing a hole in the first mate's boat.

The other two whales were harpooned, but managed to drag the boats through the waves at speed.

Back on board the *Essex*, the first mate was repairing his boat, when he felt the deck shaking.

He looked on in disbelief as an enormous whale surfaced. Not only had it deliberately rammed into the ship...

...it had turned to make a second charge.

The enraged whale darted through the waves and crashed into the wooden hull of the *Essex*.

In minutes, the ship rolled onto her side and was lost.

The harpooners released their captive whales and rowed to the rescue.

The whale pod escaped death – but only 8 men from the *Essex* survived the perilous journey home. Their amazing story inspired the novel *Moby Dick*.

Wildlife weaponry

Nature has equipped many animals with an incredible range of slashing, crushing body parts. An unarmed human is no match for these fatal weapons.

Jaws, claws and paws

Large animals can kill using powerful muscles to bite, gouge and swipe at their prey. Lions, bears and stronger animals can pierce a person's skull with their teeth, if they get close enough to bite.

Animal	Bite strength
Human	
Wolf	3x
Lion, jaguar great white shark	4.5x
Black bear, tiger	6x
Polar and grizzly bear, bull shark, gorilla	8x
Hippopotamus	12x
American alligator	14x
Nile crocodile	30x human
Saltwater crocodile	50x human

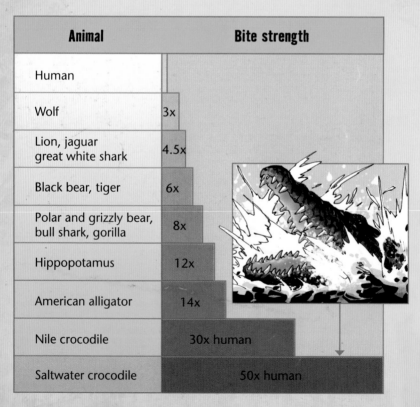

Tigers can retract their claws into their paws to protect them from snagging on the ground. Each claw can be 11cm (4.5in) long.

Chemical attack

Many animals contain toxic substances that can sicken, stun or even kill humans.

A Portuguese Man o' War looks like a jellyfish, but technically it isn't. It's a animal made up of separate creatures called *polyps* that live together as a *colony*.

Portuguese Man o' War
(Physalia physalis)

- **Distribution**: ocean surface, especially in warmer waters
- **Max. tentacle length:** 50m (160ft)
- **Human attack rate:** many thousands per year. But deaths from stings are incredibly rare.

Long tentacles are covered in parts called *cnidocysts* that inject venom.

Another polyp produces the tentacles that collect food for yet another polyp to digest.

One polyp produces a
gas-filled sail keeps the
colony afloat.

Life—threatening effects

Most animal toxins come in three main
varieties. Each is a blend of chemicals
that attack different parts of the
victim's body.

Hemotoxin

- **Example animal source**: vipers
- **Effect on body**: attacks red
  blood cells and body tissue,
  can make blood thicken,
  cause massive bleeding
  and even heart attacks.
- **Potentially lethal in**: hours

Sting or
bite wound

Neurotoxin

- **Example animal source**:
  deathstalker scorpion
- **Effect on body**: blocks
  signals between the
  brain, nerves and organs.
  Can lock muscles and so
  prevent breathing.
- **Potentially lethal in**: minutes

Necrotoxin

- **Example animal source**:
  brown recluse spider
- **Effect on body**: eats away at
  flesh and tissue, especially
  around the bite.
- **Potentially lethal in**: days

Venomous
or poisonous?

Animals can unleash
a toxic attack with
bites and stingers or
even by being eaten.

- If toxins are directly
  pumped into a
  victim using fangs,
  stingers or spines,
  they're *venoms*.

- If toxins are
  delivered after a
  victim eats or
  touches an animal,
  they're *poisons*.

Indian cobra bites cause thousands of deaths each year – often the result of people disturbing or stepping on the snakes by accident.

Too close for comfort

For humans, the most dangerous animals are not the most powerful or venomous. The risk of attack comes when people and animals are forced together in a busy habitat.

Common name

Size compared to a human being

Indian cobra

(Naja naja)

Scientific name for the type of creature

Species name

- **Distribution**: India and southeast Asia
- **Max. length**: 2.4m (8ft)
- **Human attack rate**: several thousand per year. With treatment, most victims survive.

Where it is most commonly found

How many people are attacked or killed by it each year

Largest recorded size

Devastating diseases

In the past, insects and vermin caused millions of
deaths by carrying deadly germs from one person
to another inside crowded cities.

 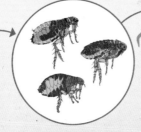 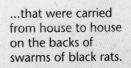

In 1665, a strain of
plague germs killed
around 100,000
people in London.

The germs were
transmitted by
blood-sucking fleas...

...that were carried
from house to house
on the backs of
swarms of black rats.

Fighting back

Nowadays, diseases such as plague can often
be prevented or treated with medication. The
effects of venom can be reversed by timely
injections of *antivenom* or *antivenin* —
although each antivenom only
works on a specific venom.

Venom comes
out through
the snake's
fangs.

A technician is 'milking'
a puff adder to get a
sample of its venom.
This helps make puff
adder antivenom.

Small but powerful

Some of the deadliest animals on Earth are no bigger than the tip of your finger. A single biting insect can kill a person. Others may attack in swarms that overwhelm a victim with hundreds of stings.

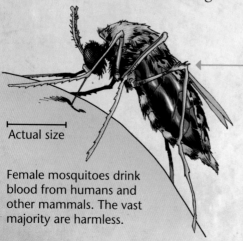

Actual size

Female mosquitoes drink blood from humans and other mammals. The vast majority are harmless.

Mosquito *(Anopheles)*

- **Main distribution:** sub-Saharan Africa
- **Max. size:** 1.6cm (0.7in)
- **Human death toll:** at least 725,000 per year

Some mosquitoes transmit germs between bite victims, causing diseases such as dengue fever and West Nile virus. One type of mosquito, the female *Anopheles*, can transmit deadly malaria germs.

Honey bee *(Apis)*

- **Distribution:** worldwide
- **Max. size:** 3cm (1.2in)
- **Human death toll:** hundreds of people every year

Although a single bee sting is rarely fatal, an entire swarm of bees can kill easily.

Around 3% of people around the world are severely allergic to bee stings. If untreated, these people may die from a single sting.

Asian giant hornet
(Gastridium geographus)

- **Main distribution:** forests and jungles of East Asia
- **Max. size:** body 5cm (2in)
- **Human death toll:** over 100 per year

Although incredibly painful, the hornet's sting is only fatal to people stung multiple times, or those with allergies.

Lonomia caterpillar
(Lonomia obliqua)

- **Distribution:** southern Brazil
- **Max. length:** 5.5cm (2.5in)
- **Human death toll:** a few people per year

Tiny bristles inject deadly venom that causes kidney failure.

Lonomia caterpillars grow up to become harmless moths.

Driver ants *(Dorylus)*

- **Distribution:** central and eastern Africa
- **Max. length (queen ant):** 8cm (3in)
- **Human death toll:** less than one person each year

Driver ants can march in colonies of 20 million individuals.

Dorylus mandibles are tough enough to pierce human skin.

Driver ants have been known to find their way inside a sleeping person's mouth and throat, and can inadvertently kill their host.

The bigger they come...

...the weaker their venom. The biggest creepy crawlies, such as tarantulas, can inject venom into victims when they bite. But smaller spiders deliver stronger, more potent toxins.

Orange baboon tarantula
(Pterinochilus murinus)
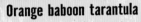

- **Distribution**: central, eastern and southern Africa
- **Max. body size**: 15cm (6in)
- **Human death toll**: none

This tarantula is shown here at actual size.

Orange baboon tarantulas are among the most vicious of all spiders. They will bite to defend themselves, as well as to attack prey.

When threatened, a tarantula will try to make itself look bigger by rearing up on its back legs and raising its front legs.

This spider's bite is more painful than a rattlesnake's bite, but its venom is far less dangerous.

These animals can kill small mammals, but have never been known to kill a human.

Eight-legged horrors

Some of the most fearsome creatures on Earth belong to a group of animals known as *arachnids*. Each has eight legs, and many have fangs or stingers that can deliver deadly venom.

Like mosquitoes, ticks can transfer diseases from a sick person to a healthy one.

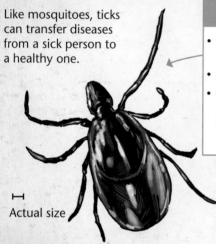

⊢⊣
Actual size

Deer tick *(Ixodes)*

- **Main distribution:** North America, northern Eurasia
- **Max. body size:** 0.3cm (0.25in)
- **Human death toll:** hundreds of people per year are infected following a tick bite, but very few die as a direct result.

Deer ticks are known to transmit Lyme disease, typhus and various other infections – all at the same time.

Sydney funnel-web spider
(Atrax robustus)

- **Distribution:** in and around the city of Sydney, Australia
- **Max. body size:** 5cm (2in)
- **Human death toll:** in the past, around 1 per decade – but none since the creation of an antivenom in 1981.

There are six different types of funnel-web spiders in Australia. Each has a potentially fatal bite.

A bite from a Sydney funnel-web could kill a human within 15 minutes. Their fangs are so sharp, they can slice through clothing and even fingernails.

This especially venomous spider has a habit of lurking in dark, tight spaces.

Brazilian wandering spider
(Phoneutria)

- **Main distribution:** South America
- **Max. body size:** 5cm (2in)
- **Human death toll:** around 7 per year

In 2005, a Brazilian wandering spider reached the UK in a crate of bananas, and bit the man who opened it.

Black widow spider
(Latrodectus)

- **Distribution:** worldwide
- **Max. body size:** 3.8cm (1.5in)
- **Human death toll:** less than 5 per year

The venom of female black widows is three times stronger than that of males.

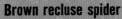

There are around 40,000 different species of spiders. Only 200 species produce harmful venom.

There are at least 32 species of black widows. All have a venomous bite.

Brown recluse spider
(Loxosceles reclusa)

- **Distribution:** North America
- **Max. body size:** 2.5cm (1in)
- **Human death toll:** none

Bites from these spiders are not fatal, but can cause severe skin decay, in rare cases requiring amputation.

Stinging tails

The deadliest arachnids are not spiders, but scorpions. Like spiders, they try to avoid contact with people, but if disturbed they can inject venom with their stabbing tails.

Indian red scorpion
(Hottentotta tamulus)

- **Distribution**: India, Pakistan, Nepal and Sri Lanka
- **Max. length**: 9cm (3.5in)
- **Human death toll:** hundreds of people are stung each year; around 40% die

Only 25 out of more than 1,500 different types of scorpions produce a venom that harms humans.

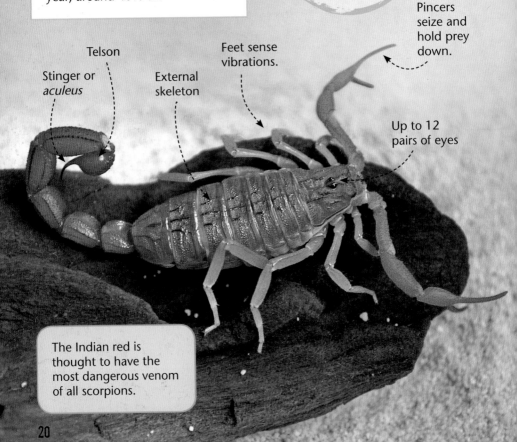

Telson

Stinger or *aculeus*

External skeleton

Feet sense vibrations.

Pincers seize and hold prey down.

Up to 12 pairs of eyes

The Indian red is thought to have the most dangerous venom of all scorpions.

Venomous scorpions typically have large tails and small pincers.

Fattail scorpion
(Androctonus)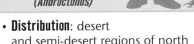

- **Distribution**: desert and semi-desert regions of north Africa and the Middle East
- **Max. length:** 10cm (3.9in)
- **Human death toll:** hundreds of people are stung each year; around 10% die

Scorpion venom is more toxic than snake venom, but causes fewer deaths. That's because most scorpions inject very little venom with each sting.

Ambush hunters

Snakes lurk under desert rocks and in jungle undergrowth, waiting to strike at passing prey – such as frogs, lizards or small mammals. No venomous snakes hunt humans, but they will bite if they feel threatened.

Their venom is powerful enough to kill a person in less than one hour.

Black mambas are believed to be the most aggressive and fastest-moving snakes of all.

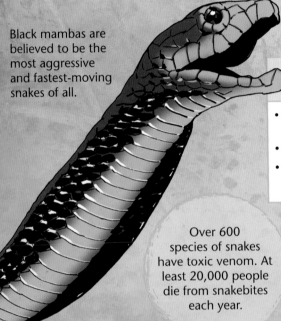

Black mamba
(Dendroaspis polylepis)

- **Distribution**: sub-Saharan Africa
- **Max. length**: 3.8m (12ft, 5in)
- **Human death toll:** At least 30 per year

Over 600 species of snakes have toxic venom. At least 20,000 people die from snakebites each year.

Vipers kill more people than any other type of snake, but only because they live in heavily populated places.

Saw-scaled viper
(Echis)

- **Distribution**: India, Pakistan, Middle East and north Africa
- **Max. length**: 1m (3ft)
- **Human death toll:** hundreds per year

Eastern brown snake
(Pseudonaja textilis)

- **Distribution**: Australia and Indonesia
- **Max. length**: 2.4m (7ft, 11in)
- **Human death toll:**
  fewer than 1 per year

Although this is one of the world's most venomous snakes, prompt treatment with antivenom saves nearly all bite victims.

Mojave rattlesnake
(Crotalus scutulatus)

- **Distribution**: southwest USA and central Mexico
- **Max. length**: 1.4m (4ft, 6in)
- **Human death toll:**
  several bites each year, but almost no fatalities

Even a dead snake should be avoided – a detached snake's head has a bite reflex, and can still inject venom.

Coral snake
(Micrurus fulvius)

- **Distribution**: southern states of USA
- **Max. length**: 1.2m (4ft)
- **Human death toll:**
  around 5 bites per year, but no fatalities since 1960.

Venomous varieties of coral snakes have touching red and yellow bands.

The serpent king

The world's largest venomous snake is the king cobra. Its fearsome fangs can inject enough deadly venom to kill an elephant.

Venomous fangs

All cobras can pump venom through their fangs. Some species can even spit the venom up to 2m (6.6ft) away.

Male king cobras are larger than females, but females can be more dangerous. Females will guard their nests closely for months, defending against potential threats to their unhatched eggs.

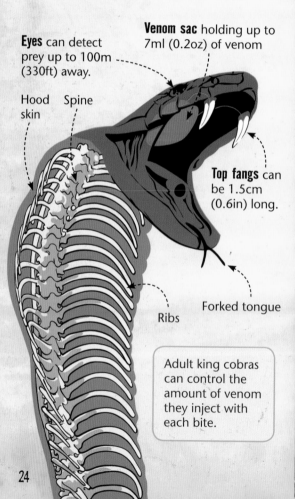

Venom sac holding up to 7ml (0.2oz) of venom

Eyes can detect prey up to 100m (330ft) away.

Hood skin

Spine

Top fangs can be 1.5cm (0.6in) long.

Forked tongue

Ribs

Adult king cobras can control the amount of venom they inject with each bite.

Rib bones in the hood help it to swell up, making the snake appear larger.

King cobra
(Ophiophagus hannah)

- **Distribution**: India and southeast Asia
- **Max. length (male):** 5.5m (18ft)
- **Max. length (female):** 3.5m (12ft)
- **Human death toll:** around 5 people per year

Its throat can produce a growling sound as a warning.

Squeeze of death

Not all snakes use venom to kill. Some of the heaviest
and most powerful snakes are *constrictors* – snakes
that squeeze the life out of their prey.

African rock python
(Python sebae)

- **Distribution**: sub-Saharan Africa
- **Max. length:** 7m (24ft)
- **Human death toll:**
  less than one per year

Rolls head over
to hold prey
upside down.

Experts are still unsure how the squeeze
kills. It is not through broken bones or
breathing prevention, but probably
because it causes a heart attack.

This python is crushing a Thomson's gazelle.

Open wide

Constrictors swallow their dead prey whole. Their jaws are connected by flexible bands that allow their mouths to open incredibly wide – wide enough to swallow a person.

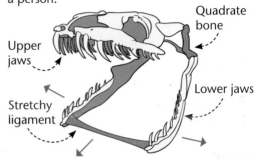

Quadrate bone

Upper jaws

Lower jaws

Stretchy ligament

1 The snake covers the head of the animal with slippery saliva, to help it slide along its gullet.

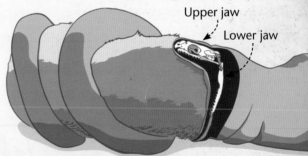

Upper jaw

Lower jaw

2 The animal sits in the snake's belly, where it is digested slowly over the next few days.

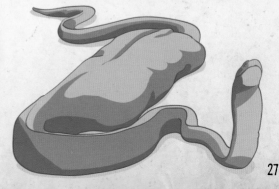

Coils body around prey and squeezes tight.

27

Deadly animals under threat:
Indian subcontinent

With their ice-locked mountain ranges and steaming jungles, India and the countries in south Asia are home to a startling range of big cats, venomous snakes and other wonders of nature.

Most animals shy away from people, but ever-expanding cities mean that even the hardiest are running out of room to survive.

Common krait
(Bungarus caeruleus)

- **Distribution**: in almost any habitat in and around India
- **Max. length**: 1.75m (5ft, 9in)
- **Human death toll:** at least 100 per year

Kraits are night hunters and are active in cities as well as rural areas. Their bites can be almost painless, until the effects of their venom take hold.

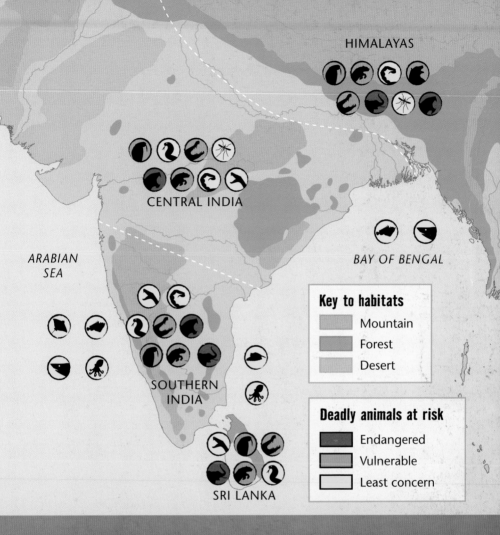

HIMALAYAS

CENTRAL INDIA

ARABIAN
SEA

BAY OF BENGAL

SOUTHERN
INDIA

Key to habitats

Mountain
Forest
Desert

Deadly animals at risk

Endangered
Vulnerable
Least concern

SRI LANKA

Deadly animals on land

 Indian cobra
 Crocodile

 Black bear
 Tiger

 Leopard
 Mosquito

 King cobra
 Common krait

 Asian elephant
 Indian red scorpion

Deadly animals at sea

 Stonefish

 Blue-ringed octopus

 Tiger shark

 Stingray

 Cone snail

Land of dragons

Most lizards are timid creatures, no bigger than your hand. But one rare species can grow to a terrifying size – the Komodo dragon. This animal lives wild on just five islands: Komodo, Rinca, Flores, Gili Motang and Padar, all part of Indonesia.

Komodo dragon
(Varanus komodoensis)

- **Distribution**: southern islands of Indonesia
- **Max. length**: 3m (10ft)
- **Max. weight**: 70kg (150lbs)
- **Human death toll**: only a few people every hundred years

Tracking a scent

Like many reptiles, the dragon has a long, forked tongue to aid its sense of smell.

If a scent is stronger on one fork, the dragon will head in that direction, helping it to track its prey.

Komodo dragons have up to 60 teeth, all with serrated edges, and venom that kills slowly.

One other lizard is sometimes thought of as a hazard – the gila monster.

Powerful jaws grip tightly and produce a painful but non-lethal venom.

Gila monster
(Heloderma suspectum)

- **Distribution**: southwestern USA and northern Mexico
- **Max. length:** 60cm (2ft)
- **Human death toll:** no deaths reported for over 60 years

Sharp claws can rake through skin.

Tough scales protect against most attacks.

American alligator
(Alligator mississippiensis)

- **Distribution**: rivers and swamps of southeastern USA
- **Max. length**: 4.6m (15ft)
- **Attacks on humans**: at least five per year, most are non-fatal

Huge, powerful tail propels crocodilians through water around three times as fast as human swimmers.

Locking an animal between its jaws, a crocodilian will quickly drag it under water to drown it.

Alligators and crocodiles cannot chew food with their snapping jaws. Instead, they grip prey with their teeth and spin their bodies, breaking a kill into small chunks to swallow.

Swamp lurkers

Crocodilians – crocodiles, alligators and caimans – are found across the world, often in tropical waters. Crocodiles are some of the only animals that actively hunt humans as prey.

Crocodiles and alligators can be distinguished by their teeth and snouts.

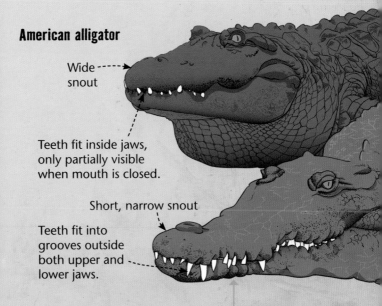

American alligator

Wide ----▸
snout

Teeth fit inside jaws,
only partially visible
when mouth is closed.

Short, narrow snout

Teeth fit into
grooves outside
both upper and ----▸
lower jaws.

Saltwater crocodile
(Crocodylus porosus)

- **Distribution**: swamps, lagoons and rivers of southern Asia and northern Australia
- **Max. length**: 6.7m (22ft)
- **Human death toll**: around 10 per year

In the jaws of death

DATE: February 1985

LOCATION: Kakadu National Park, Northern Territory, Australia

BACKGROUND: Ecologist Val Plumwood was canoeing along a lonely stretch of the East Alligator lagoon – home to many fearsome saltwater crocodiles.

Kakadu National Park

AUSTRALIA

Plumwood believed she was safe in her 5m (16ft) canoe...

...but grew increasingly nervous when she spied what appeared to be a log in the water.

Before she could paddle away, the 'log' – in fact a hungry crocodile – smacked into her canoe.

She made a daring leap for a branch overhanging the lagoon...

As the animal struck blow after blow, Plumwood feared her canoe would capsize.

...only for the crocodile to jump out of the water with jaws wide open.

Plumwood found herself pinned inside the animal's crushing jaws.

Three times, the croc plunged beneath the surface, rolling Plumwood in a dizzying churn of black water.

Each time, Plumwood managed to break free to catch her breath.

After the third dive, the crocodile released Plumwood, and she scrambled painfully up the bank.

She was eventually rescued by a park ranger who had gone to look for her.

Later on, Plumwood insisted that the crocodile was not to be hunted and killed – and it may still be alive today.

Pack hunters

Since ancient times, wolves have stalked lonely forests and remote places. In most cases, they try to avoid contact with humans, but an encounter with a wolf pack can have deadly consequences.

Grey wolf *or* **Gray wolf**
(Canis lupus)

- **Distribution:** wilderness areas of the northern hemisphere
- **Max. length:** 1.6m (5ft, 2in)
- **Max. speed:** 70km/h (44mph)
- **Human death toll:** fewer than 100 per year

Body shape is designed to cope with rough terrain and thick snow.

Legs are built for stamina, and can maintain high speeds over long distances.

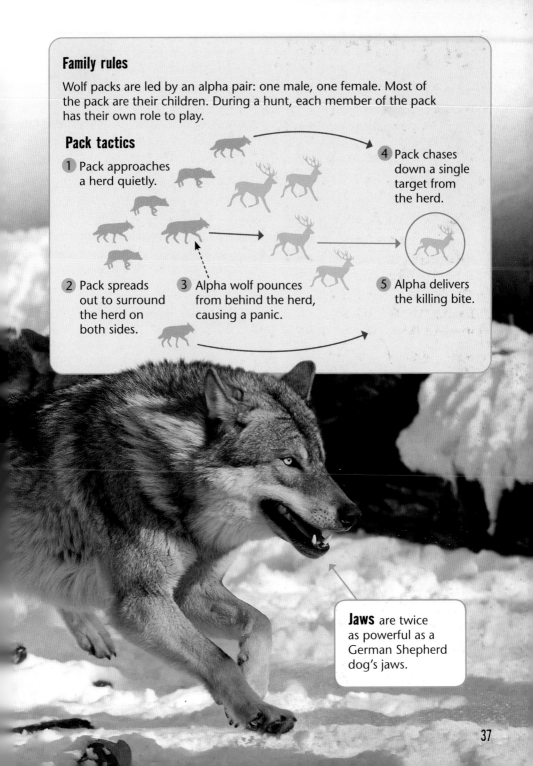

Family rules

Wolf packs are led by an alpha pair: one male, one female. Most of the pack are their children. During a hunt, each member of the pack has their own role to play.

Pack tactics

1 Pack approaches a herd quietly.

2 Pack spreads out to surround the herd on both sides.

3 Alpha wolf pounces from behind the herd, causing a panic.

4 Pack chases down a single target from the herd.

5 Alpha delivers the killing bite.

Jaws are twice as powerful as a German Shepherd dog's jaws.

On the prowl

Many of the big cats are *apex predators* – carnivores too strong to be threatened by other species. Their patience, speed and power make them among the deadliest of all land animals.

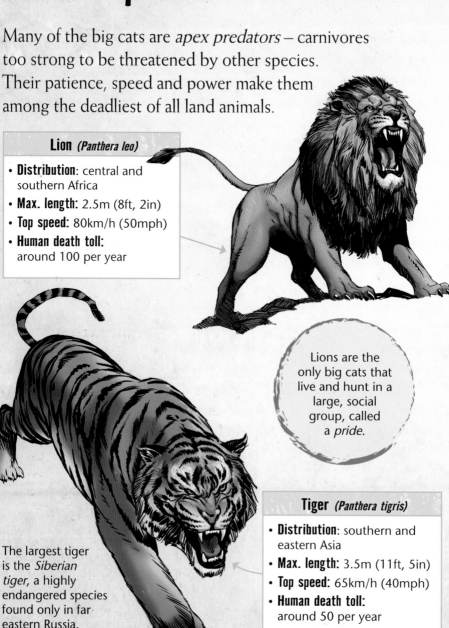

Lion *(Panthera leo)*

- **Distribution**: central and southern Africa
- **Max. length**: 2.5m (8ft, 2in)
- **Top speed**: 80km/h (50mph)
- **Human death toll**: around 100 per year

Lions are the only big cats that live and hunt in a large, social group, called a *pride*.

The largest tiger is the *Siberian tiger*, a highly endangered species found only in far eastern Russia.

Tiger *(Panthera tigris)*

- **Distribution**: southern and eastern Asia
- **Max. length**: 3.5m (11ft, 5in)
- **Top speed**: 65km/h (40mph)
- **Human death toll**: around 50 per year

Cheetah (*Acinonyx jubatus*)

- **Distribution**: central and southern Africa
- **Max. length:** 1.5m (5ft)
- **Top speed:** 120km/h (75mph)
- **Human death toll:** less than 5 per year

Cheetahs have incredible grip, a streamlined body shape and a flexible spine. These natural advantages make them the fastest animals on land.

Cougar (*Puma concolor*)

- **Distribution**: North and South America
- **Max. length:** 2.75m (9ft)
- **Top speed:** 80km/h (50mph)
- **Human death toll:** less than 5 per year

Jaguars and leopards sometimes have black fur. These varieties are often called *black panthers*.

Jaguar (*Panthera onca*)

- **Distribution**: central and South America
- **Max. length:** 1.9m (7ft)
- **Top speed:** 80km/h (50mph)
- **Human death toll:** less than 3 per year

Tigers have the strongest mouth grip, but jaguars can bite down with greater force – enough to pierce a turtle shell.

Stealth hunter

Leopards hunt at night, silently stalking their prey before making swift, savage attacks. Like all big cats, they use keen senses and powerful muscles to catch animals up to three times their own size.

A single creature, dubbed *the leopard of Panar*, is believed to have killed 436 people in the Almora district of India in the 1900s.

Tail bones are used for balance, and to help the cat change direction mid-jump.

Spine and shoulders can flatten to the ground to help the cat hide in the grass.

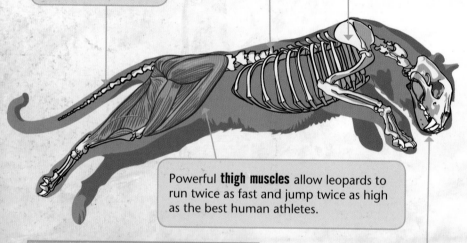

Powerful **thigh muscles** allow leopards to run twice as fast and jump twice as high as the best human athletes.

Strong **jaws** can kill by biting through the throat or crushing the skull of prey.

Leopard
(*Panthera pardus*)

- **Distribution:** Africa and southern Asia
- **Max. length:** 1.9m (6ft, 3in)
- **Max. speed:** 60km/h (37mph)
- **Human death toll:** less than 50 per year

Leopards often hide their kills from scavengers. This leopard is about to jump down after retrieving a kill concealed in a tree.

Hearing
is up to five times better than a human's. Ears can swivel to help pinpoint source of sounds.

Paws
are large and broad to spread the weight of the cat and help it move silently.

Night vision
is up to seven times better than a human.

Cats' eyes are designed to let in lots of light. A layer of tissue on the retina also lets some light bounce back...

Pupil

Retina

...allowing light sensors to pick up extra information. This makes cats' eyes seem to glow when a light shines on them.

Claws
are long and strong, used for climbing trees as well as attacking prey.

Duel in the jungle

DATE: 1926

LOCATION: Rudraprayag, northern India

BACKGROUND: For eight years, the people of Rudraprayag lived in fear of a maneating leopard. Local reports claim it had killed 125 people in that time.

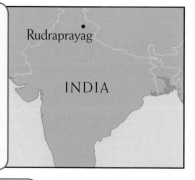

Rudraprayag

INDIA

Hunting only at night, the leopard would even smash through doors or windows to reach its prey.

Once, the leopard broke into a room that was holding 40 goats.

But the maneater had developed a taste for human flesh.

It didn't eat a single goat, preferring to eat the human goatherd, who had fallen asleep.

The locals called in a specialist hunter – Jim Corbett – famed for killing over a dozen tigers and leopards. He set a trap at the edge of the jungle.

Corbett hid in a tree

Goat (bait)

Bell

After ten nights in the tree, Corbett was ready to give up. He decided to make one last vigil...

...and, soon after dark, the goat's bell began to tinkle.

Corbett flicked a flashlight on and pulled the trigger on his rifle.

DING DING

Corbett waited until sunrise to follow the leopard's trail. He found it lying, dead, in a dip in the ground.

Corbett continued to work as a hunter of maneating animals. By the time he retired in 1938, he had killed 33 of them, saving thousands of lives.

River wild

Tropical rivers and lakes can appear to be still and peaceful places, but they are home to some terrifying animals.

Massive jaws and black scales for camouflage make the caiman a deadly night hunter.

Red-bellied piranha
(Pygocentrus nattereri)
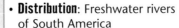

- **Distribution**: Freshwater rivers of South America
- **Max. length:** 33cm (13in)
- **Human death toll:** very few confirmed fatalities

Piranhas swim in schools of up to 100 fish, enough to devour a lone swimmer.

Anacondas lurk in the bushes near riverbanks, before wrapping themselves around passing animals and killing them.

Green anaconda
(Eunectes murinus)

- **Distribution**: northern South America
- **Max. length:** 6m (20ft)
- **Human death toll:** very few confirmed fatalities

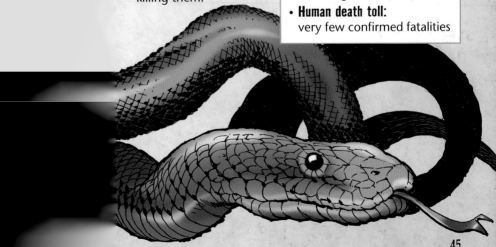

Deadly animals under threat:
American jungles

The lush, Amazon rainforest teems with an incredible variety of animal species – many of them deadly. A combination of logging, mining and deforestation is putting some of these species under threat of extinction.

Mini–killer

One of the deadliest animals on Earth is a tiny frog. Known as the golden poison frog, it exudes an incredibly powerful toxin through its skin.

There are several species of poison frogs; sadly many of them are in danger of extinction.

A single frog holds less than a teaspoonful of poison – but this amount is powerful enough to kill more than 10 people.

Actual size

Golden poison frog
(Phyllobates terribilis)

- **Distribution**: rainforests of Colombia
- **Max. length**: 5.5cm (0.3in)
- **Human death toll:** less than 5 per year

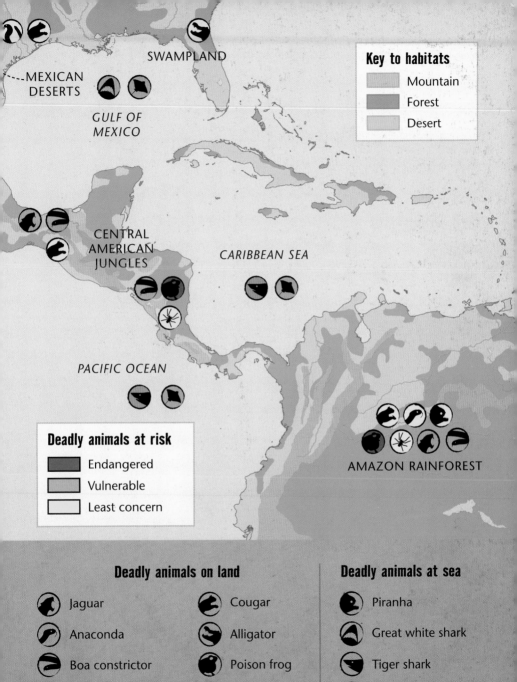

SWAMPLAND

MEXICAN DESERTS

GULF OF MEXICO

Key to habitats

	Mountain
	Forest
	Desert

CENTRAL AMERICAN JUNGLES

CARIBBEAN SEA

PACIFIC OCEAN

Deadly animals at risk

	Endangered
	Vulnerable
	Least concern

AMAZON RAINFOREST

Deadly animals on land

- Jaguar
- Anaconda
- Boa constrictor
- Wandering spider
- Cougar
- Alligator
- Poison frog
- Rattlesnake

Deadly animals at sea

- Piranha
- Great white shark
- Tiger shark
- Stingray

47

King of the forest

Brown bears live in forests and mountain areas across the northern hemisphere. They may attack people when surprised or to defend their cubs. Any bear can easily outpace a human – and kill one with a single swipe of its paw.

A brown bear will rear up on its hind paws to smell the air or get a better view of its surroundings.

North American brown bears are often known as *grizzly bears*. The largest of all brown bears is a variety of grizzly called the *Kodiak bear*.

Brown bear *(Ursus arctos)*

- **Distribution**: northern Europe, northern Asia, and North America
- **Max. length**: 2.8m (9ft, 2in)
- **Human death toll**: around 10 per year

Black bear *(Ursus americanus)*

- **Distribution**: North America
- **Max. length**: 2m (6ft, 7in)
- **Human death toll**: one or two per year

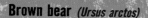

Super sense

This woodland hunter has a sensory area for picking up a scent that is 100 times larger than a human nose. This helps it sniff out prey from more than a mile away.

Hearing and vision are as strong as a human's.

Shoulder hump holds muscles that power the bear's paws, making it a strong digger and deadly swiper.

Claws are each as long as a human finger.

The undersides of each paw are covered in tiny bumps that provide a strong grip.

Polar giant

Polar bears are the largest land predators on Earth. These colossal animals live and hunt across the Arctic ice plains, surviving in one of the world's harshest climate zones.

Polar bear
(*Ursus maritimus*)

- **Distribution:** Arctic regions of USA, Canada, Russia and Scandinavia
- **Max. length:** 3m (10ft)
- **Max. speed:** 40km/h (25mph) on land 10km/h (6mph) in water
- **Human death toll:** less than one per year

Nose can follow the scent of a seal from over 1.6km (one mile) away.

Paws can be as wide as dinner plates, helping the bear spread its weight over thin ice.

Arms are powerful enough to knock a person's head off.

Paws serve as paddles in the water, making polar bears excellent swimmers.

Kesagake the killer

DATE: December 1915

LOCATION: Rokusen-sawa village, Hokkaido, Japan

BACKGROUND: In November, a brown bear awoke early from hibernation. Desperate for food, it broke into a food store, ate crops and scared off a horse.

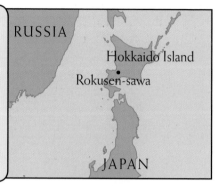

RUSSIA

Hokkaido Island

Rokusen-sawa

JAPAN

One morning in early December, the bear smashed its way into a home belonging to the Ota family.

The woman inside struck the bear with firewood, but was killed along with a child.

Sure that the bear would strike again, the villagers set a trap. Fifty armed guards hid in a house belonging to the Miyoke family, not far from the Ota house.

Ota home

The bear was soon spotted by the Ota home again. The armed guards charged at the bear, firing their guns and chasing it into the forest.

The bear was cunning. It lost the guards among the trees...

Bear's route

Guard's route

Miyoke home

Shots fired

Ota home

...and returned to attack the women and children left at the Miyoke house.

Desperate for help, one of the villagers found a retired hunter named Yamamoto.

The killer bear must be *Kesagake*.

I hunted him some years ago, but he escaped.

Guards surrounded the house, but the bear burst out and escaped after causing a panic.

Two days later, Yamamoto and another hunter found the bear's tracks.

They followed the tracks to a clearing, and shot Kesagake in the heart and the head, killing him.

Shaken by the attacks, the villagers abandoned Rokusen-sawa. It remains ghostly and deserted to this day.

Deadly defenders

Some of the most dangerous animals aren't maneaters or even carnivores, but will kill to protect their territory. Massive and unpredictable, they can trample and crush unwary people to death.

Hippo
(Hippopotamus amphibius)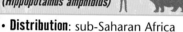

- **Distribution**: sub-Saharan Africa
- **Max. length**: 5.2m (17ft)
- **Max. weight**: 3,200kg (7,100lbs)
- **Human death toll**: 100-500 per year

Hippos attack animals and people who enter their section of river.

Asiatic rhino
(Rhinoceros unicornis)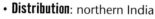

- **Distribution**: northern India
- **Max. length**: 3.8m (12ft 6in)
- **Max. weight**: 4,000kg (8,800lbs)
- **Human death toll**: around 10 per year

Asiatic rhinos are not as large, or as aggressive, as African rhinos – but they cause more deaths.

African *or* Cape buffalo
(Syncerus caffer)

- **Distribution**: sub-Saharan Africa
- **Max. length**: 3.4m (11ft)
- **Max. weight**: 900kg (2,000lbs)
- **Human death toll:**
  around 200 per year

Human deaths caused by gigantic plant-eating animals far outnumber deaths caused by maneating carnivores.

Buffalo herd together to protect their young from predators. They are untameable, and are one of the most aggressive species in Africa.

Deadly defenders: elephants

Elephants are the largest and most powerful land animals. They are not carnivores, but they use their trunks, tusks and immense strength to protect their herd and young.

Asian elephant
(Elephas maximus)

- **Distribution:** India and southeast Asia
- **Max. height:** 3.3m (11ft)
- **Max. weight:** 8,000kg (17,600lbs)
- **Human death toll:** up to 300 per year

Elephants can attack people if they threaten their habitats. Although smaller, Asian elephants cause many more human deaths than African elephants.

Trunk is powerful enough to rip trees from the ground; can hold up to 300kg (660lbs).

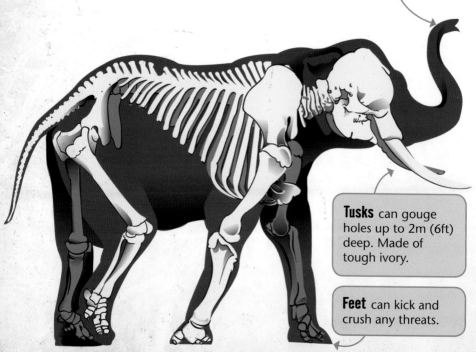

Tusks can gouge holes up to 2m (6ft) deep. Made of tough ivory.

Feet can kick and crush any threats.

African bush elephant
(Loxodonta africana)

- **Distribution**: Central Africa
- **Max. height:** 4m (13ft)
- **Max. weight:** 10,000kg (22,000lbs)
- **Human death toll:** less than 100 per year

When excited or agitated, an elephant will flap its ears. Elephants can hear warning sounds from herd members many miles away.

This African bush elephant is warning the car to back off.

Shuffling feet is a sign of aggression.

African elephants are much larger than Asian elephants, and just as deadly. But because they live in more remote areas they cause fewer deaths.

XZZ 763 GP

DISCOVERY 3

Deadly animals under threat:
Sub-Saharan Africa

This vast region of grasslands, jungles and mountains is birthplace to some of Earth's most amazing animal species. Illegal hunting is widespread across Africa's national parks and wildlife areas, threatening even the deadliest animals.

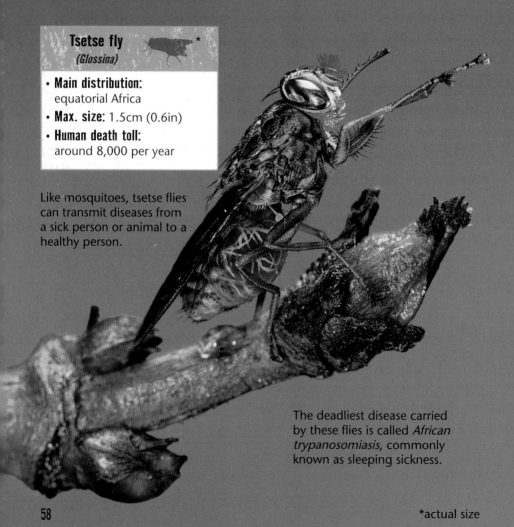

Tsetse fly *
(Glossina)

- **Main distribution:** equatorial Africa
- **Max. size:** 1.5cm (0.6in)
- **Human death toll:** around 8,000 per year

Like mosquitoes, tsetse flies can transmit diseases from a sick person or animal to a healthy person.

The deadliest disease carried by these flies is called *African trypanosomiasis*, commonly known as sleeping sickness.

*actual size

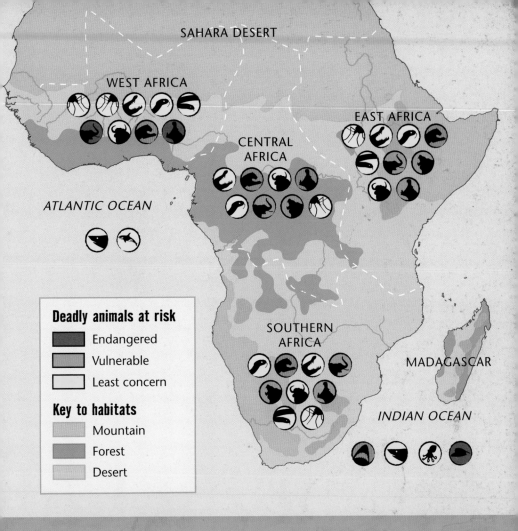

SAHARA DESERT

WEST AFRICA

EAST AFRICA

CENTRAL AFRICA

ATLANTIC OCEAN

Deadly animals at risk

- Endangered
- Vulnerable
- Least concern

Key to habitats

- Mountain
- Forest
- Desert

SOUTHERN AFRICA

MADAGASCAR

INDIAN OCEAN

Deadly animals on land

 Puff adder
 Anopheles mosquito
 Black mamba
 Tsetse fly
 Crocodile

 Lion
 Leopard
 African elephant
 Hippopotamus
 Cape buffalo

Deadly animals at sea

 Cone snail
 Killer whale
 Bull shark
 Great white shark
 Blue-ringed octopus

59

Seas of death

Sharks and killer whales are big, ocean-roaming predators, but there are many smaller creatures living in the deep that are just as dangerous, thanks to their powerful venom.

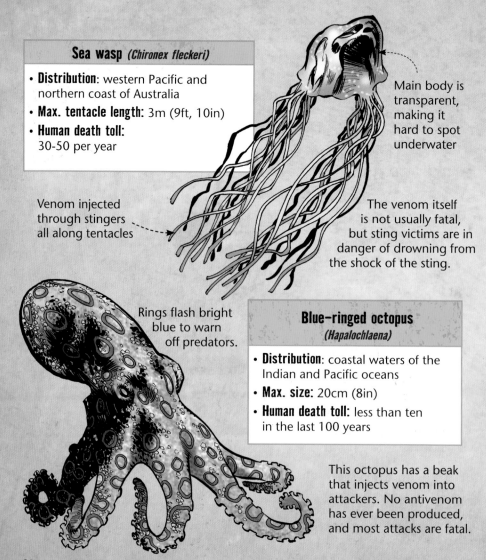

Sea wasp *(Chironex fleckeri)*

- **Distribution**: western Pacific and northern coast of Australia
- **Max. tentacle length:** 3m (9ft, 10in)
- **Human death toll:** 30-50 per year

Main body is transparent, making it hard to spot underwater

Venom injected through stingers all along tentacles

The venom itself is not usually fatal, but sting victims are in danger of drowning from the shock of the sting.

Rings flash bright blue to warn off predators.

Blue-ringed octopus
(Hapalochlaena)

- **Distribution**: coastal waters of the Indian and Pacific oceans
- **Max. size:** 20cm (8in)
- **Human death toll:** less than ten in the last 100 years

This octopus has a beak that injects venom into attackers. No antivenom has ever been produced, and most attacks are fatal.

Cone snail
(Conus)

- **Distribution**: all across tropical waters
- **Max. length**: 15cm (6in)
- **Human death toll**: only a few per year

Venom injected by needle-sharp tooth

A whip of this tail is strong enough to break bones.

Long tail with razor-sharp barb that injects venom into victims.

All cone snails have toxic venom; the largest species can be lethal.

Whiptail stingray (Dasyatidae)

- **Distribution**: tropical waters
- **Max. length**: 2m (6ft, 6in)
- **Human death toll**: several attacks per year but very few deaths

Stonefish (Synanceia)

- **Distribution**: tropical coasts of Indian and Pacific Oceans
- **Max. length**: 60cm (24in)
- **Human death toll**: only a few in the last ten years

Venom injected through spines all over its back.

Body is naturally camouflaged on the stony sea bed.

Perfect predators

The waters of the Earth teem with over 470 distinct species of sharks. Tracking prey with incredible senses, all sharks can propel themselves at impressive speeds – like torpedoes with teeth.

Great white sharks are the largest sharks, and cause more human deaths than any other variety.

Pectoral fins
control depth.

Caudal fin steers
the shark.

Great White shark
(Carcharodon carcharias)

- **Distribution**: worldwide in warm, shallow coastal waters
- **Max. length**: 6.4m (21ft)
- **Max. weight**: 3,300kg (7,300lbs)
- **Max. speed**: 60km/h (37mph)
- **Human death toll**: a few per decade

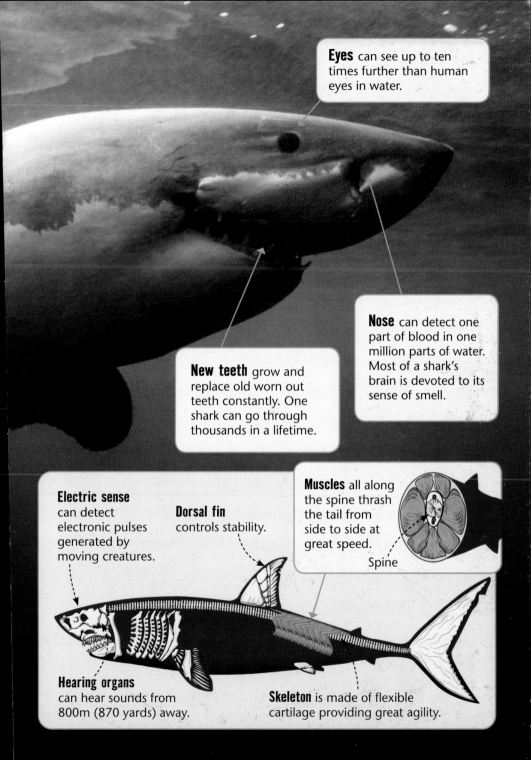

Eyes can see up to ten times further than human eyes in water.

Nose can detect one part of blood in one million parts of water. Most of a shark's brain is devoted to its sense of smell.

New teeth grow and replace old worn out teeth constantly. One shark can go through thousands in a lifetime.

Electric sense can detect electronic pulses generated by moving creatures.

Dorsal fin controls stability.

Muscles all along the spine thrash the tail from side to side at great speed.

Spine

Hearing organs can hear sounds from 800m (870 yards) away.

Skeleton is made of flexible cartilage providing great agility.

Single-minded killers

All species of sharks are designed with one main aim: to kill. They do not target humans as prey, but the biggest ones may attack people if they smell blood.

Young tiger sharks have distinctive stripes on their skin.

Tiger sharks will eat almost any animal, from turtles to birds to people.

Tiger shark
(Galeocerdo cuvier)

- **Distribution**: warm and tropical waters, especially coastal areas
- **Max. length:** 5m (16ft)
- **Human attacks:** around 5 per year, rarely fatal

Whitetip sharks are known to follow ships at sea. They are believed to have killed more people than any other shark species, although the number of attacks has fallen as more people travel by air than sea.

Oceanic whitetip shark
(Carcharhinus longimanus)

- **Distribution**: warm and tropical waters, especially out at sea
- **Max. length:** 3m (9ft, 10in)
- **Human attacks:** very few in the last 50 years

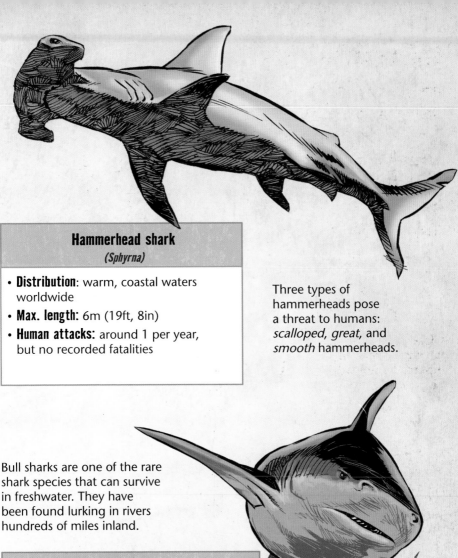

Hammerhead shark
(Sphyrna)

- **Distribution**: warm, coastal waters worldwide
- **Max. length:** 6m (19ft, 8in)
- **Human attacks:** around 1 per year, but no recorded fatalities

Three types of hammerheads pose a threat to humans: *scalloped*, *great*, and *smooth* hammerheads.

Bull sharks are one of the rare shark species that can survive in freshwater. They have been found lurking in rivers hundreds of miles inland.

Bull shark
(Carcharhinus leucas)

- **Distribution**: worldwide in warm, shallow oceans and rivers
- **Max. length:** 2.5m (8ft)
- **Human attacks:** a few each decade, with some fatalities

Sperm whale
(Physeter macrocephalus)

- **Distribution**: worldwide in seas and oceans
- **Max. length:** 20m (65ft)
- **Human death toll:** none reported in the last 100 years

Despite an impressive array of huge teeth, sperm whales don't often bite their prey – they swallow them whole.

Lords of the sea

Mighty and majestic, great toothed whales prey on deepwater squid and even sharks, but only rarely harm people.

Killer whale
(Orcinus orca)

- **Distribution**: worldwide, more often in coastal areas than in open sea
- **Max. length:** 9.8m (32ft)
- **Human death toll:** no known deaths have been caused by wild orca, but very occasionally orca in captivity attack their handlers.

Clever killers

DATE: January 1911

LOCATION: McMurdo Sound, Antarctica

BACKGROUND: Photographer Herbert Ponting was part of a team led by British polar explorer, Captain Scott.

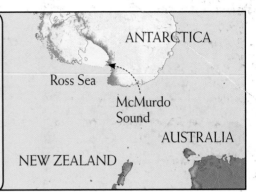

ANTARCTICA

Ross Sea

McMurdo Sound

AUSTRALIA

NEW ZEALAND

Ponting spotted a killer whale by the edge of an ice floe. He moved closer to take a picture...

...only for a second whale to ram the ice beneath his feet, breaking the floe into pieces.

Ponting struggled to keep his balance as the whales nudged his ice island...

...trying to knock him into the water.

By chance, a sea current pushed Ponting's floe to the shore and he jumped to safety.

"I looked back," Ponting wrote later in his diary, *"and I saw the terrible teeth which I had so narrowly escaped."*

Deadly animals under threat:
Australian wilderness

Ringed by wild oceans and with a harsh, desert interior, Australia can boast an exceptional collection of deadly species. But it's also one of the safest countries to live in. Expert medical teams save nearly all animal attack victims.

Dingoes are cousins to wolves. They often attack farm animals, but only rarely approach people.

Pure dingoes are a dwindling species, because of interbreeding with domestic dogs.

Dingo
(Canis lupus dingo)

- **Main distribution:** deserts and grassland of Australia and southeast Asia
- **Max. length:** 1.5m (5ft)
- **Human attacks:** less than 1 per year, and only rarely fatal

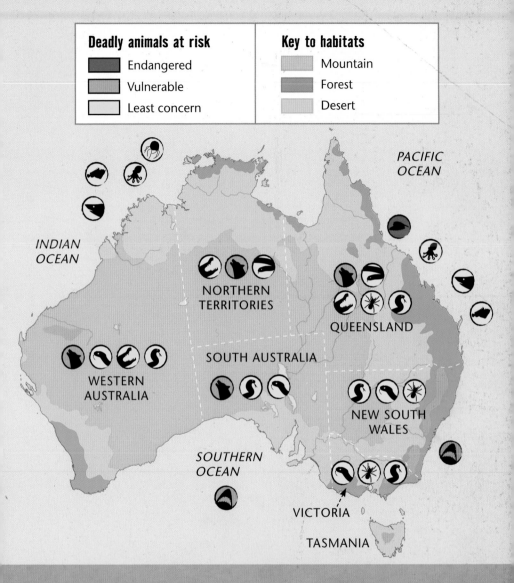

Deadly animals at risk

- ■ Endangered
- ■ Vulnerable
- □ Least concern

Key to habitats

- Mountain
- Forest
- Desert

PACIFIC
OCEAN

INDIAN
OCEAN

NORTHERN
TERRITORIES

QUEENSLAND

SOUTH AUSTRALIA

WESTERN
AUSTRALIA

NEW SOUTH
WALES

SOUTHERN
OCEAN

VICTORIA

TASMANIA

Deadly animals on land

 Dingo

 Funnel web spider

 Saltwater crocodile

 Tiger snake

 Taipan

 Eastern brown snake

Deadly animals at sea

 Box jellyfish

 Blue-ringed octopus

 Stonefish

 Cone snail

 Great white shark

 Bull shark

To be confirmed

Scientists and explorers discover new animal species every year. It's possible that a host of legendary, deadly animals, known as *cryptids*, do exist – they're simply hiding in the wildest places on Earth.

Monsters of the deep

Barely 5% of the world's ocean wilderness has been explored. If there are any genuine cryptids left to discover, it's likely they live deep underwater.

Tentacles of doom

For centuries, sailors told tales of huge, tentacled beasts strong enough to splinter large ships. They had no hard evidence for these monsters, which they named *giant squids*.

But, in 2004, a film crew captured images of these 12m (40ft) long animals in deep water off Japan.

The study of mysterious or unproven animals is called *cryptozoology*.

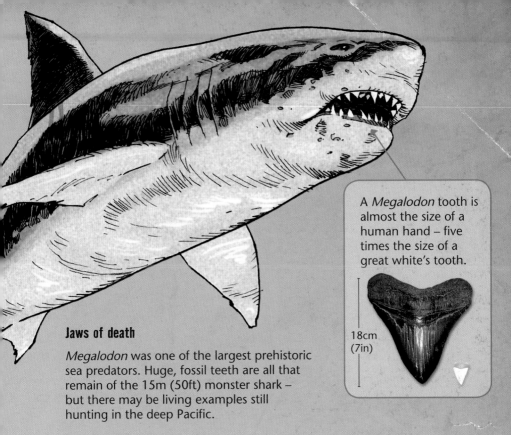

Jaws of death

Megalodon was one of the largest prehistoric sea predators. Huge, fossil teeth are all that remain of the 15m (50ft) monster shark – but there may be living examples still hunting in the deep Pacific.

A *Megalodon* tooth is almost the size of a human hand – five times the size of a great white's tooth.

18cm (7in)

Mountain man

Stories of a tall, ape-like animal living in the Himalayas have been common for centuries. Some cryptozoologists claim this creature, known as the *Yeti*, or *Abominable Snowman*, is a lost relative of the polar bear.

33cm (13in)

Explorer Eric Shipton took pictures of tracks he found on Mount Everest in 1951.

Park rangers are airlifting this rhino to a remote area far from any poachers.

A blindfold helps to keep the animal calm.

Call of the wild

Many deadly species are losing their feeding grounds and habitat to new towns and the world's growing population. Vets and rangers work to safeguard animals from illegal hunters and protect their wilderness homes.

This bus takes photographers into bear territory. Huge wheels and high windows keep the tourists out of a bear's reach.

Close encounters

Watching wild animals in their native habitat is a breathtaking experience.

Photographers and adventurers use special safety equipment to get within touching distance of the most deadly creatures on Earth.

A fighting chance

Animal attacks are rare. In fact, far more people survive encounters than die – but quick medical treatment is essential to improve your survival chances.

Read on for other key survival tips...

Every year, around 1.3 million people are killed in road traffic accidents; far more than are killed by wild animals.

Mosquito bite

- **Method of attack**: a bite anywhere on the body, that may transmit killer viruses into the bloodstream.
- **Kill speed**: months
- **Survival chance**: good
- **Survival tip**: precautionary malaria tablets combined with hospitalization helps most victims recover completely. The most serious malaria infections kill up to 20% of victims, even with treatment.

Snake venom

- **Method of attack**: a bite to the hand or foot, often with an injection of venom into the flesh.
- **Kill speed**: hours
- **Survival chance**: good
- **Survival tip**: identify or even photograph the snake, so that the correct antivenom can be administered.

Shark's teeth

- **Method of attack**: a bite to the leg or side
- **Kill speed**: seconds
- **Survival chance**: likely
- **Survival tip**: a shark will often release its victim after the first bite, giving the opportunity to escape to shore and medical help.

Crocodile roll

- **Method of attack**: jaws grip onto the victim's body, then the animal rolls underwater, hoping to shock, stun or drown the victim
- **Kill speed**: minutes
- **Survival chance**: poor
- **Survival tip**: a crocodile will sometimes release its victim after the first roll, affording an opportunity to escape.

Bear attack

- **Method of attack**: a swipe of the paws that causes massive injuries, or a bite to the head that can crack open a human skull.
- **Kill speed**: seconds
- **Survival chance**: minimal
- **Survival tip**: black bears can be scared off by loud noises or people standing tall. The only hope against a brown bear is to play dead.

The deadliest of all

With our growing population, horrific weapons and ongoing damage to our environment, no other species comes close to the destructive potential of human beings.

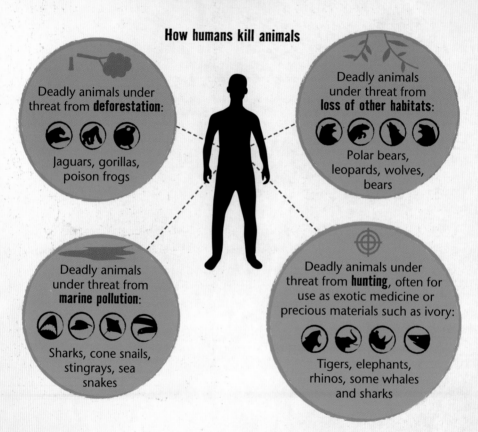

How humans kill animals

Deadly animals under threat from **deforestation**:

Jaguars, gorillas, poison frogs

Deadly animals under threat from **loss of other habitats**:

Polar bears, leopards, wolves, bears

Deadly animals under threat from **marine pollution**:

Sharks, cone snails, stingrays, sea snakes

Deadly animals under threat from **hunting**, often for use as exotic medicine or precious materials such as ivory:

Tigers, elephants, rhinos, some whales and sharks

Making amends

As more people experience the thrill of getting close to creatures in the wild, we are beginning to understand how vital it is to protect animals and their habitats.

Glossary

This glossary explains some of the words used in this book. If a word is written in *italic* type, it has an entry of its own.

allergy A severe reaction to a *toxin* that can be fatal.

alpha The lead animal in a group, such as a wolf or lion.

antivenin Another word for *antivenom*.

antivenom A drug that reverses the effects of an animal's *toxic* attack, also known as *antivenin*.

apex predator A *predator* that is not itself hunted by any other animal in its normal *habitat*.

arachnid A type of animal with eight legs, including spiders and scorpions.

bristles Small, animal hairs.

carnivore An animal that only eats other animals.

conservation Work done to protect animals and their natural *habitat*.

constrictor A type of snake that kills by tightening its coils around its *prey*.

crocodilians A group of reptiles that includes crocodiles and alligators.

death roll A rolling, underwater attack used by a crocodile.

endangered Word for a species in serious danger of becoming *extinct*.

extinct No more living examples of this species are known to exist.

habitat The overall living space of an animal in the wild.

maneater An animal that preys on humans.

poison A *toxin* produced by an animal that can be passed on to an attacker indirectly, for example if the animal is eaten or touched.

predator An animal that hunts and kills other animals for food.

prey Any animal that is hunted, killed and eaten by a *predator*.

ranger An animal expert and warden who works at a natural park or wilderness reserve.

scavenger An animal that eats *prey* killed by other *predators*.

shark cage A metal cage that protects people swimming close to sharks.

toxin Any chemical produced by an animal that can cause harm to a human or other animal.

venom A *toxin* that is injected into the bloodstream of an animal, often by biting or stinging.

Index

Acknowledgements

Every effort has been made to trace and acknowledge ownership of copyright. If any rights have been omitted, the publishers offer to rectify this in any future editions following notification. The publishers are grateful to the following individuals and organizations for permission to reproduce material on the following pages:

cover Saltwater crocodile near Darwin, Australia © Peter Walton photography / Getty images; **p1** Polar bear in Hudson Bay, Canada © Paul Souders / Corbis; **p2-3** © Jeff Rotman / Getty images; **p4** © William Ervin / SPL; **p9** © Toni / Getty images; **p10** © Stephen Frink Collection / Alamy; **p12** © Lynn M. Stone / NPL; **p13** © Anthony Bannister / Gallo Images / Corbis; **p16-17** © C. Steimer / Picture Alliance /Photoshot; **p20** © Aaron Saguyod; **p21** © Ovia images / Alamy; **p24-25** © Sanjeev Gupta / epa / Corbis; **p26-27** © Nigel Pavitt / Getty Images; **p28** © DEA / Dani-Jeske / Getty Images; **p30-31** © Mike Lane / FLPA; **p31** (top) © Rick & Nora Bowers / Alamy; **p32-33** © Robert Seitz / Imagebroker / FLPA; **p36-37** © Christoph Bosch / Alamy; **p41** © Beverly Joubert / Getty images; **p46** © 2 / Bjorn Holland / Ocean / Corbis; **p48** © Morales / Getty images; **p50-51** © Bethany Helzer / Getty Images; **p54-55** © Theo Allofs / Corbis; **p57** © Our Wild Life Photography / Alamy; **p58** © Kim Taylor / NPL; **p62-63** © David Fleetham / SeaPics; **p66** (top) © WaterFrame / Alamy; (bottom) © Frans Lanting / Mint images / Getty Images; **p68** © Robin Hausmann / Imagebroker / FLPA; **p71** (top) © Jeff Rotman / Getty images; (bottom) © Topical Press Agency / Getty Images; **p72** © Pete Oxford / Minden Pictures / Corbis; **p73** © Doug Allan / Getty images.

Deadly animals on the internet

For links to websites where you can watch video clips of deadly animals in the wild, read true stories of dangerous encounters, and find out how you can help worldwide organizations protect endangered species, go to the Usborne Quicklinks website at **www.usborne.com/quicklinks** and enter the keywords: **deadly animals**.

Additional illustrations by Tom Lalonde and Helen Edmonds
Series editor: Jane Chisholm   Series designer: Zoe Wray
Digital design by John Russell   Picture research by Ruth King